Salt Water Reflections

Melody Mann

BookLeaf
Publishing

Presentation by *BookLeaf Publishing*

Web: www.bookleafpub.com

E-mail: info@bookleafpub.com

ISBN: 9789357440080

First edition 2023

To the man who taught me how to take my first steps - rest easy mamaji. May you find serenity in open waters once more.

ACKNOWLEDGEMENT

Heartfelt gratitude to my family, friends, and loved ones who helped me see this literary journey through. Despite my hesitations and confusion, you all stayed by my side as I completed this poetic endeavor. I appreciate each and every one of you for being the community that keeps me going.

PREFACE

Salt Water Reflections is a limited debut poetry collection, capturing the essence of the ocean. Together with the help of nature, we explore the organic parts of ourselves in this journey. Written next to the open waters on the island of Oʻahu in Hawaiʻi, this collection captures the flow of movement and recognition. Life presents us with a plethora of continuous change. By understanding the power of loss, noticing the strength in resilience, and celebrating the efforts of healing, this poetic encounter will leave you nourished and grounded. Follow along these pages at your own pace to capture a unique individualized experience. Allow the words to bounce off you if needed and resonate deeper when called for to digest the messages. These words will sing a different song to each of you; listen carefully.

Grounding Practice

This is a letter from the ocean which stretches
infinitely -
A humble reminder of the natural aura ever
surrounding,
Gentle nudges to return to the organic.

Go ahead and seek shelter ashore,
Feel the warmth trickling down as it coats the
skin's surface in soft golden hues,
Relish the sand swirling between the toes amid
the incoming current's strength,
Watch as the waves lazily lapse against the
shins-
sending cooling chills up the legs which alert the
conscious mind,
Listen to the air whispering a song of solitude to
the ears,
For the sea salt, sunshine, and open waters
welcome you home; sensory recollections.

Acceptance

The waves hum a solemn tune to listening ears,
& as the sun sets in the horizon the sky begins to
melt into hues of closure,
the universe is unveiling its true colors -
mystifying the night with rich shades of
realization and composure,
A journey shared once is now one she treads
alone,
Her footprints forming a solitary trail in the sand
as she encounters the path before her,
He is nowhere to be seen -
rather a memory to be felt;
An ache to remember.

Maya

Constant motion stirring within the tides,
Shifting currents pushing and pulling the
inevitable,
Lost among such mayhem searching for footing,
Lifted and afloat bending to natural will,
An endless pursuit of impermanence;
maya (illusion).

More

If I could turn back time and sit with you a
moment more,
My the stories we would explore,
Possibilities stained with infinite hues would
dance amid our conversations,
To lock in the actuality of me and you,
A forever would be short at the
creator's hand,
Everything would have been novel - vibrant -
and grand,
Such lonesome quarrel as I ponder and dream,
Mortality is fickle - leaving such fragmented
visions; salutations.

Trance

Uplifted from the moment your soul transcended
past the horizon,
Our mortal skies began to melt into saturations
beyond ordinary compositions,
This realization casted shades of envy and
separation,
For we had nothing left but to lay basking in the
eminent glory of life's natural order,
Although lonesome eyes remain peering beyond
that which the mind can fathom,
May the beauty of impermanence remain
sovereign.

Haste

Your silence echoes in her mind's chamber,
A harsh halt to the infinite possibilities that once
danced before her,
Sudden yet sadly expected - what felt feverish
ended in haste,
Mistaken for thinking for her you knew naught
of what she held within,
Unspoken secrets now released to the open
winds,
Heavy truths float freely as they whisper her
broken desires to scattered palm leaves,
Rooted in memory and growing with resilience;
time will tell.

Discord

Shared laughter melts into fond memories,
Joint mayhem of anxiety filled productivity
amounts to bittersweet gratitude at year's end,
Together what sparked now dulls at a discord of
sorts,
To pause and hit rewind would be a serene
becoming,
Alas a continuous exchange of stop and go will
be the reality dealt,
Missing the familiar.

Borrowed Time

Imperfections in the actions and the words
woven,
Apologies dismantled at noontide,
Sifting through currents on borrowed time -
veering into the inevitable,
A margin so subliminal that the only hues of
redemption linger in hindsight,
Monotonous thoughts swirl and wash over with
confusion,
An ultimate reckoning rests on such
benevolence,
Sincere pleas fall silent in presence of actuality;
a salutation paused.

Within

With each sunrise they beaconed a new calling,
Illuminating their surroundings together their
laughter filled rooms with contagious glee,
Brightening even the dullest days with happiness
and sunshine,
For even uncertainty began to look promising,
How unforgiving time is that the impermanence
of our experiences are sealed with each passing
hour,
To remind us of the joys vested within moments
shared,
To remind us of time together is sacred and
cherished,
For the sun will set and they'll be seated to
harbor upon inner turmoil;
Gracious memories personified.

Farewell

Goodbyes are bittersweet,
Symbolic of shared memories and heartfelt
unity,
Of rough patches and turmoil,
Of celebrations and good times,
Of tears and anxiety,
Of happiness and peace.

Goodbyes are bittersweet,
A lingering hope for another moment more,
A plea for permanence,
For amid such departure the heart pines,
Goodbyes are bittersweet,
Often unexpected and abrupt,
It leaves one to question reality and ponder fate,
For closure is not promised and words are left
unspoken,
The fear of being forgotten,
The weariness of separation.

Goodbyes are bittersweet,
They loom in the forecast awaiting to release the
self from attachment,
Natural and unforgiving in nature,
An ending no one prepares for,

A feeling consuming to process independently,
An inescapable journey.

Goodbyes are bittersweet,
Farewell.

Suicide Awareness

A song ending mid verse leaves an audience
pleading for the remaining symphony,
When joyous laughter filling a room silences it
casts a shadow of internal remorse,
A clock expiring prematurely hardens the core,
These incompletes give birth to a frenzy of
emotions,
These incompletes create a bundle of questions
left unanswered.

Allow your song to play each and every melody
despite the discord in its composition,
Laugh wholeheartedly as you enter new spaces
and allow your voice project strongly,
Leave the clock alone for time shall run its
natural course at its own pace,
Lean in and trust in the universal cues
surrounding you.

You are safe in this moment,
Although hardships may weigh heavily on the
mind - hold onto the promise of tomorrow;
nevertheless keep persisting.

Five Stages

She runs to the park aimlessly as she lost all
sense of direction,
Perched upon the play structure she hides in
elementary nostalgia,
Seeking refuge from the realities of adulthood.

The news of his leap met her ears in disbelief -
denial began to shield her heart,
Surely such tragedies cannot be warranted on
short notice?
They must be mistaken, what do police know
anyway?

Her guard rises abruptly and she surges across
the playground in anger,
How could someone end their path before it ever
truly began?
Why wouldn't he reach out when he had the
chance to today?
She was right there. Distant, but there.

She settles into the swing and begins bargaining
to universal cues,
Pleading for a moment more to just turn back
time and relish such presence,

To spare her from a life of regret as she holds
onto unspoken emotions,
As she now has to cling to hidden sentiments;
It wasn't supposed to be this way.

Met with deafening realization that the
inevitable had dawned - depression snares her in
its lure,
Swaying on the swing in monotonous motions
her body numbs,
Her thoughts swirl,
Her mind goes blank;
He really decided to quit.

Realizing one cannot force the hands of fate she
watches the sunset with acceptance,
The atmosphere sends chills down her spine as
the present moment greets her,
Today will never be the same as yesterday,
An era of change has arrived,
She begins a journey of resilience and
persistence.

Getting up from the swing she leaves the park
and play structures behind,
Growing past elementary nostalgia; becoming.

Alone, not Lonely

Surrounded by solitude she sits atop coarse
warm granules,
Cool waters tease her toes as she allows the
waves to wash up against her legs,
Sunshine beams against her face bringing light
and patience to her consciousness,
Such simplicity vested in these moments where
she ventures to the beach alone,
Armed with a pen and journal she begins to
unravel stifled truths,
Inking realizations and memories on bounded
pages,
Sharing recollections with confessions across
these open spaces,
A meditative practice of releasing the self,
For just as souls remain singular in their arrival
and departures - so does she venture alone to pay
homage to higher origins,
She treads this path alone, not lonely.

Reclaiming the Self

Letting go never felt so thrilling,
Embrace the uncertainty of tomorrow -
let loose in this moment,
Leave your expectations to float freely in the
open seas,
Set sail on a voyage inward,
Connect with your intuition and relinquish these
mortal cycles,
Rise to new revelations and release angst,
Make intentional spaces for your healing,
Reclaim the self.

Rewind

If I could repeat this life there would
be much to do,
Hearts to mend and deeds to undo,
Time spent mustering courage would transform
into acts of expression,
My journal would be blank for my prose would
meet your ears and not the page,
I would share my mind's cavern with you and
the journey would be ours to conquer,
If I could rewind and reverse time,
I'd relish this life with you.

Hopeful

Sunlight begins peeking through the clouds at
daybreak,
Hope slowly cascades throughout the foyer,
Although once renounced - this space is now a
haven you may retreat to,
You are safe to inhabit and make this your own,
Learn to accept each passing day as a blessing,
Savor the taste of solitude as it dances upon such
pursed lips,
Tomorrow is hidden in a haze but today in
indefinite,
In light of what has become relish the potential
of what can be,
Let your spirituality ground you to find yourself
again; trust.

Forever Friend

A companion through the seasons you
welcomed our every phase,
From rising triumphs to deafening cries,
You stood alongside us through the mayhem,
Whilst humanity is fickle and forevers aren't
certain,
You were the constant that prevailed,
Alas at summer's end you submerged with the
currents,
Washing away opportunities of relishing
tomorrow's sunlight,
Submerging in infinite radiance you rejoin the
promised,
Memories strike annually of your departure;
a forever friend.

Flow

Uplifting her conscious she surpasses the limits
of boundaries defined,
She gains clarity and stillness within the
moment,
The path before her isn't linear for it is scattered
with bends and trials
Uncharted glories in both grief and love,
Realized potential for her to readily embrace,
A turbulent hesitation softened at nature's
reassurance,
Steady she treads at a new pace through the
notions of life;
Continuous flow.

Becoming

Enter effortlessly into life's oasis for the waters
are still,
Allow the universe to unfold this new reality
that welcomes your becoming,
Such eternal calls soften to the weary and
embrace the tiresome,
You are a reservoir of potential and abundance,
Simmer down and float in the omnipresence of
the present,
Flow courageously but at your own strides,
For this too shall pass.

Beyond

Find solace in remembering we are not of this
world - rather that of light,
We are merely visiting the grand scheme of
nature,
A light peeking through the darkness of illusion,
The striking silence amid a discord of melodies,
We belong to a comfort felt by omnipresent
energies,
A home stretching further than that which meets
the eye;
A drop of the celestial current.

Submerge

The ocean is home to a myriad of creatures and
vegetation,
The waters harbor secrets sealed and fluid only
to lunar splendors,
For these saline droplets hold the memories of
the departed,
A vessel that houses the ashes of the lost,
The vault preserving treasures of the forgotten,
An entity coexisting with the dreams of the
wishful,
The ocean is a graceful being;
submerge yourself.

www.ingramcontent.com/pod-product-compliance
Lightning Source LLC
Chambersburg PA
CBHW070731160726
48003CB00006BA/2442